Down In the Dumps... *Get Pumped Up*

Your Inspiration guide to a new found peace

By

Prologue

This is your first step, to your road to recovery. The first step is always the hardest, but we must start somewhere. I'm glad you chose this route to find your new found peace; even if you feel like you already have a fairly peaceful life.

In this book you will be required to face your challenges head on, no matter what the circumstances may be. No, it won't be easy, but it will be well worth it in the end. This is not a book you breeze through, as if it is a novel. Just like anything else, it takes time to make a change, and this journey will be no different. Take your time, and allow the process to take effect.

Throughout this journey you will find motivation quotes and scriptures to help you along this journey. This book is based on events, trials, and tribulations I have experienced throughout my own life, and now I want to share with you. It's time to take life by the horns, and start living your purpose. God gave you a purpose to fulfill and now it's time to start doing so. No more making excuses or procrastinating, as to why you can't have a peaceful life, or take this journey. Today is the day to start making a change and find your new found peace. Get out of those dumps, and start getting pumped up. Remember...You can do all things through Christ who strengthens you. Now let's start this journey to a new found peace.

Finding an intimate relationship with God

Embrace yourself in his arms, and all your troubles
will be gone

To find an intimate relationship with God does not
mean you have to go to church every day, or read your bible
every day. When I was growing up, I was taught that in order to
go to heaven I had to go to church. If I didn't go to church, I was
surely going to hell. For many years I felt like this, until the day I
had the ultimate wakeup call from God. When God wakes you
up, you know you are being awakened.

Over the years, I had to learn and understand what it
meant to have an intimate relationship with God. You see, the
relationship I have with him will not be the same relationship
you have with him. You have to learn how to become one with
him, how to talk to him, how to listen to him. There are so many
levels to this that we would have to write a whole other book to
cover it in detail. However, I'm going to give you a few pointers
on how you can have an intimate relationship with God.

Before I go on, I know some of you read my motivation
quote and felt all kinds of ways. You only felt like that, because
you don't have an intimate relationship with God. When you

have an intimate relationship with him, no matter what you're going through; nothing can throw you off your game. The relationship I have created with God, allows me to know that as long as I embrace myself in his arms all my troubles are gone. Once you find your intimate relationship with him, you will eventually feel the same way.

Here are a few helpful tools, to help you find an intimate relationship with God.

Prayer- In order to pray, you have to learn how to talk to God. Get rid of the crazy thoughts, that there is a certain way to talk to God. No it's not. God asks that you come to him honestly. When you talk to God, you talk to him as if he's your friend, your brother, your confident. When you talk to him, you never have to worry about your business being talked about in the streets or the church. God will always hold and keep your deepest secrets; although, he already knows. He wants to hear it from you. Don't be afraid to open up, and let it all go; not just when you're hurting. He wants you to talk to him when you're happy, sad, confused, angry, or tired. No matter what you're going through, he just wants to be a part of your life.

Praise- Have you ever felt like you wanted to run around, and scream and shout? That's how you give praise. However, you have to be willing to do the same thing; even when you're going through the storm. It's easy to praise God and thank him when things are great, but can you do the same thing when things aren't going so great? In order to find your peace, you must learn how to praise him through the storm. This was the hardest thing I had to learn. So many times I had to ask God, "How can I praise you, when my heart is so heavy?" I know you may have felt like this many times. For me, I had to practice praise. Yes it's true, practice does make perfection. Every day I open my eyes, I say thank you; that's giving God praise. Every time you bring God up in your conversation without thought; that's giving God praise.

These simple things to add to your daily routine should be easy enough for you to handle. Sometimes, we feel like we have to go all out, but I'm here to tell you; less is more. You don't have to go over and beyond to give him praise, but you do have to put it in your daily routine. If you deny him in front of your friends, he will deny you in front of his father.

When you love God the way he loves you, there is nothing that can keep you from praising his holy name. Having an intimate relationship with God will help you find your new found peace. So what are you waiting for?

Taking Your First Step

Step on your fear, and stand out on your faith

Taking your first step is always the hardest, but someone has to do it; shouldn't it be you? So many times we stand in our own way, and never realize how many blessings we block, or how many opportunities we miss. If fear is holding you back from doing what you love to do, it's time to step on your fear and stand out on your faith.

For so long, I was looking for my purpose in all the wrong places. When the entire time, I was scared to step out on my faith and do what God was calling me to do. My purpose was to be an author, a motivational speaker, and spread the goodness of God by any means necessary. In the beginning of my journey, I was scared. I was so scared that I started asking other people what I should do. Have you ever done that before? I'm pretty sure you have. We've all done that a time or two in the course of our lives and some of us do it more often than others.

People laughed in my face when I shared my dreams with them, and some said that I would never amount to anything. Now look at me. I am living my dreams, and building my empire. Yes, I still have a ways to go, but I refuse to allow anything to stand in the way of my dreams and goals.

Today is the day for you to make the first step. Step out of your comfort zone, and start living your purpose. Don't allow people to validate who you are, or tell you what you can't do. In Philippians 4:13 (KJV) The bible teaches us that we can do all things through Christ who strengthens us. It's time to know that God will guide you through, if you put your trust in him. He doesn't give you the tools you need, if he didn't want you to use them.

There are so many things we allow to stand in our way of being able to take that first step. When I decided to become a writer, I had to put all my trust in God. I didn't know where to start, or how to begin. I would reach out to people, but people would never respond. I could've stopped there, and allowed people to make me quit. I could've used my sickness as an excuse, to not begin my journey. If you're using that as an excuse, stop right now. No matter how sick you are, you have to create a job for you; it's something you must be good at. You have to find what you're good at, and make it work for you. You don't have to have a college degree to get started, or any of that. All you have to do is have the will to take the first step, and know God will carry you through.

Here are a few helpful tips to help you take the first step.

Make a list- making a list may sound easy, but in reality; it's not. It takes time to create this list. This list will allow you to get in touch with you. It will have you facing your reality. Once you create your list, you can't stop there. See, life is always revolving and changing, and we must change with it. This is how we grow.

Your first list should consist of these columns:

- Dreams
- Goals
- To do list (How you reach your dreams and goals)

If you are past this point and you are trying to make a first step in other areas of your life; your list should consist of these columns:

- What you want
- What you don't want
- What you will not accept

These are the main two lists I keep somewhere I can see every day. Life can be so complicated, that it's easier to reach your goals, if you have something you can relate back to. Now don't try to put everything on the list. Remember...it will change over time. Only choose the top ten things and work from there. As you successfully complete each item on your list, cross it off and rate your success. Once you've completed the list, continue with your next session and so forth. Over time, you will see your growth within you.

Believe in you- It can be fairly hard to believe in ourselves. Why? Because, we are our worse critics. We talk ourselves out of more things than just a little bit. Always telling ourselves that we are not good enough, or we are not worthy. You have to ask yourself, how can you not be good enough, or worthy if God made you in his own image. It's time to rebuild and find your strength. You have a voice, but you have to believe in yourself.

When I decided to go into radio in 2013, I was scared out of my mind. I had told myself so many times that no one would listen to my show, or take me seriously. Here I am five years later, still doing the same thing. The one thing I was scared of doing, I trusted God to carry me through and now I'm heard all over the world. I didn't know Fast Life On the Move would be a success, or anything else I did for that matter.

Yes taking the first step was hard, but I stood on my fear and stepped out on my faith. In James 4:8 (NKJV) it states "Draw near to God, and he will draw near to you."

So what are you waiting for? If you take one step, he will take ten. All you have to do is believe and trust in **YOU**.

Loving You First

In order to love anyone else, you have to love you
first

Every day, we scream and shout we love ourselves, but
deep down inside we are falling apart. Putting on a smile,
making everyone believe you are okay. When in reality, you're
really not. Deep down you are lost and confused, abused and
battered, neglected and rejected. How many times have you felt
this way? This is a feeling I know oh too well. I've felt this way,
and probably more; I haven't even listed.

People seem to think it's easy to love you, when it's
really not. It's hard to love ourselves because some of us really
don't know what love really is. You may have come from a
broken home, maybe even have an abusive background; so how
can you truly know what love is, if you've never received it?
You're probably thinking to yourself that there's no way in the
world that's possible. Yeah, for a long time I thought the same
way; until, I understood God's unconditional love. Once you
embrace God's love, you will know and understand the true
meaning of love.

I didn't always receive the love I wanted, so love was
just a pun to me. Something I heard of but didn't quite believe.
The one person who actually ever showed me love, God took
from me; that's how I felt at the time. I was so angry, and

confused as to why he would take the only person who truly loved and cared for me away. I was bitter and angry with God. It was one day; I was lost and about to give up that God came and rescued me from myself. I didn't realize I was causing myself harm. I kept blaming God and everyone else around me. When in reality, God was trying to teach me a lesson; and that was how to love me.

Even through the lesson, I thought I still loved me; until the next lesson came, and that was marriage. Being married taught me a lot of things about myself. One of those things were; I was giving all my love to man, and I forgot about me. I started becoming bitter and angry all over again, and couldn't figure out why. It was at that point, I realized I loved my husband so much that I felt as if I couldn't live life without him. It wasn't because he was good to me, or that we had the perfect marriage. It was the fact that I had this idea of marriage, and thought if I gave him all of me and all the love I had to give; he would love me unconditionally, but boy was I wrong. One day, God had to show me; I had put all my trust and love in man that I forgot about him; which in turn, forgot about me.

In John 3:16 (KJV) God teaches us how to love us the way he loves us. "For God so loved the world that he gave his only begotten Son, that whosoever believeth in him should not perish, but have everlasting life."

Now if God loved us enough to sacrifice his own son for us, don't you think you should love you the same way?

Here are a few helpful tools that will help you, to start loving you.

Get in tune with you- In order to start loving you, you have to get in tune with you. Often times we think we know ourselves, but in reality we don't. We just know what we are accustomed to; which simply means, our lives have become routine. It's time to break the routine within you. No one can do this for you. Here are some questions you should ask yourself.

- **Who am I?** - You will never know who you are if you don't dig deep. You must be honest with you.
- **What do I enjoy doing?** - Now this question may be a little more difficult. Maybe you haven't done much in your life to know what you enjoy doing; so, you have to think of this another way. Ask yourself if you could do anything what would it be, and then go from there.
- **What changes do I want to make within me?** - Now understand, this is not about the outside. Look deep and find out what things about you that you would like to change. This is about growth.
- **Am I comfortable in my own skin?** - Now this is about the inside and the outside. If you are not comfortable in your own skin, ask yourself why. What are the things that make you uncomfortable when you look at yourself in the mirror? If you don't like what you see, then make the first step to change those things. Remember...Beauty is only skin deep. You don't need cosmetic surgery, or wear a lot of makeup to be beautiful. Maybe you are uncomfortable

with your weight, find ways to lose a few pounds. You don't have to be a size two, to be beautiful. I have friends that are a size twenty-two and are beautiful as can be. There are possibilities sitting at your finger tips. Google is your friend.

Prayer- Throughout this journey, you will see the word **prayer** a lot. In order to have a clearer understanding about us, we have to go to prayer. We have to ask God, to show us how to love us the way he loves us. Its okay, to ask more than once. Again, this is building your intimate relationship with God. Over time, with practice you will find yourself loving you more, and becoming more in tune with you.

Keeping Your Word with Yourself

Today I promise to be a better me, no matter what the world throws at me

Have you ever promised yourself that you were going to do something, but you never did?

Every day we make promises to ourselves that we never keep. We tell ourselves, we are going to be rich. How many of us can honestly say that we are rich? Some of us tell ourselves that we are going to start our own business, but we never do. Like most children, we have big dreams and said we were going to be an astronaut, fireman, policeman, doctor etc. How many of us can actually say that we did that? We also said we were going to buy our parents a house, and they would never have to work again. Can you say that you have done that? Many of us can't, but those were promises we made that we didn't keep.

It doesn't always have to be a big promise, but it's the little ones that we don't keep either. For example, I will not allow people to abuse me anymore. I will go to school tomorrow. I will not accept rejection. See, these are promises. They may not be as big, but none the less, they are still promises, to ourselves that we just don't keep.

For a long time, I broke many promises to myself and occasionally still do. I'm not perfect, but when you face your reality, you understand and notice when you break a promise to yourself. It's okay to be afraid to touch new heights. We are all scared at something in our lives. However, you can't keep allowing fear to stand in your way of doing what you want to do.

Now, don't go all extra with your promises. Start off small and gradually work your way up. You have to take one step at a time. Once you complete one promise, you can move on to something else.

If you can't keep a promise to yourself, there is no way you can keep a promise to others. If you do, than you truly don't love you. How can you keep a promise for others but not yourself? **Reality check**!!!

Numbers 30:2 (KJV) If a man vows a vow to the Lord, or swears an oath to bind himself by a pledge, he shall not break his word. He shall do according to all that proceeds out of his mouth.

This doesn't only mean keeping promises to other people, but if you open your mouth and make a promise to yourself, you should keep it according to God's word.

Questioning the Sanity

I may hear the voices in my head, but it doesn't mean I'm going insane

Do you ever feel like you are going insane, but don't know why? Maybe, you ask yourself why more than you should. Life is not easy, and some of our lives are more hectic than others; especially, when we have to balance a career, children, spouse etc.

This sounds like so many of us, and we often ask ourselves why we continue to do this, or when will we ever have time for us.

So many times I wanted to quit and give up; yell, scream and walk away, but I couldn't. How would my house run, if it has no order? What would my family do without me? This is a need of wanting to be needed. So many of us suffer from this and never realize it. I had to realize in order to find time for me; I had to learn how to balance all of the things going on in my life. However, that was still not enough. I still felt as if everyone depended on me. That's when I had to start breaking free. Now I know you're wondering how do I break free when my life is so complicated? It's not as difficult as we make it to be. The reality of it is, we have to start making those around us take accountability for their own lives. We can guide them and show them how to live a better life, but we can't do it for them.

If we are busy doing everything for everyone else, what will they have to do?

That's a strong question, and made you really think about it. In order to have a new found peace, we must allow people to live their own lives.

Now I know this may be easier said than done, but it can be done. You have to stop being so controlling, bossy, or nosey, and start concentrating on you. I know that may have stung a little bit, but that's facing your reality.

Our nose problem, often times cloud our better judgment. If you have a nose problem, you have to learn how to mind your own business. For their business, is not your business; so, why are you worried about what they have going on?

As parents, we often time want to control our children, and then cover it up by saying, "I'm looking out for their best interest." When in reality, you just want to make sure they are doing what you want them to do. If you are the controlling parent, first you have to realize that you are controlling. Here are a few signs to say; you are controlling.

- You do everything for your child/children- cooking, cleaning, laundry, hair etc.
- You don't like any of their friends- girlfriends or boyfriends
- They are married, yet you still want to tell them how to manage their household.

Now, I know that may have been hard for you to swallow, but it's something that you needed to hear.

We can question the sanity all day, but in all honesty, we are not insane; we just have a lot on our plates. Now is the time for you to start clearing off your plate. Once you can allow the people you love to start living their life, so you can start living your life.

I understand it's hard to live your life when your children or family is all you have. However, this goes back, to getting in touch with you. In order to break the cycle, you have to know who you are as an individual. You can't live your life through them. You have to live your life for you.

If you don't feel like cleaning up on that day, then don't. Who says you have to? If your children or family can't understand that, then maybe it's time for them to start pitching in and taking up some of the slack. They are not entitled to live in a clean house, if they refuse to help out. They are not entitled to have clean clothes, if they refuse to do their own laundry.

Now, if it's you that's stopping them from taking care of them; shame on you. You can't complain about doing anything, when you are simply doing it to yourself.

There are so many parts to questioning the sanity, but the bible teaches us that God doesn't put more on us than we can bear.

1 Corinthians 10:13 (ESV) No temptation has overtaken you that is not common to man. God is faithful, and he will not let you be tempted beyond your ability, but with the temptation he

will also provide the way of escape, that you may be able to endure it.

So see, you can escape from your insanity and find a new peace. There is nothing that you can't ask for that God won't provide; if it's for you.

You are not crazy, you are living in a chaotic world of yourself and it's time to break free from you. You have to want to live your life abundantly, like God said you could. Why not start today? It's time to take your life back, and enjoy your family; not feel like you are Cinderella for your family. It's okay to love them, and help when you can. However, they have to learn how to take care of themselves; so you don't have to feel like you are being taken for granted, as you question the sanity of your mind.

Once I learned how to make my family be accountable for them, I found that I had more time to focus on me and do the things that actually matter to me. Every now and then, I still want to take control, but I stop myself dead in my track and make them figure it out on their own; this includes my husband. He's grown and knows how to do everything I can. I had to make him start standing up, and being the man I know he can be. There is no more relying on me to do everything for him. Yeah, there's time he tries to make me feel guilty; but it doesn't work anymore. I stand my ground, and make him do it himself. Now don't think for one minute that when it's over, part of me want to get up and do as he's asked, but I don't move and I ask God to make me be still. Yes, that's my controlling, nurturing side. However, I acknowledge that this is who I am, and this part of me, I want to change. When you are aware of these things, you can change these things.

In my testimony, you see I acknowledge my weakness; which simply means, I faced my reality. I asked God to keep me still; that's my intimate relationship with God. I stood my ground; I loved me enough to put me first. I didn't want to feel like I was being used, or unappreciated by my family or husband.

In order to find your sanity, you have to follow the steps before this chapter. If you haven't grasped the concept, keep practicing. It will eventually come to you. We are different in our own way. It may take you longer to grasp everything and that's okay. As long as you're putting in the work and trying, it will eventually sink in. Never give up on you or your sanity. If you are not in your right mind, you are no good to you or anyone else. Don't allow anyone to take that away from you; no matter what situation you may be in.

Your mind is a gateway, and the devil has so many avenues when you allow him into your mind. When you stay in prayer he has no avenues to walk, because God is keeping you covered.

You are not crazy, and don't allow anyone to tell you anything differently. That's the devils way of entering into your gateway.

Today, we bind him up and rebuke him in the name of Jesus.

Facing your Reality

Looking in the mirror I see an image of me. I didn't realize it was going to make me face my reality

Life can sometimes feel, as if we're looking in a two way mirror. Sometimes we are, but we refuse to see the person looking back at us.

Throughout this journey, you have heard me say several times to face your reality. Well what does this reality look like? You may ask. This is an outlook on your life. This is a reflection of you that you often try to block. You can't block reality; no matter how hard you try. It's still going to be there, and it's still going to look the same. It will never change.

You've heard the saying, "A leopard never changes its spots," well that's what reality is. It's often cold and brutal and hard to swallow.

When I start taking my journey on a road to peace, it was hard for me to face my reality. I was the girl who thought she had it all together, and everyone loved me. I thought I was untouchable, and could do and say anything I wanted and people would accept it. Sadly, that was not the case. I was not facing my reality. I was only seeing things for what I wanted them to be. The truth of the matter is, people were talking about me in privacy of each other, but smiling in my face.

People didn't really believe in me, like I thought they did. People were not loving me, because I was a good person, they were only doing what they had to do, to get what they could; sex, money, company, etc.

Once I started facing my reality, I found myself becoming more humble. I realized that people didn't owe me anything. I owed myself to be honest with myself, and start taking a look at myself.

Doing this allowed me to see that I was dying on the inside and masking my true feelings. I was not happy with myself. I started looking back over my life and realized all the damage I had caused. Thinking people owed me something. Thinking I was all of that and a bag of chips. When in reality, they could never see me for me; because I couldn't see myself. How was I supposed to expect people to treat me like I wanted to be treated, when I was mistreating myself? We never want to face the fact that we hurt ourselves more than anyone could ever do. We are our worst enemy. I wish this wasn't so, but it's the truth.

Once you start facing your reality, it's easy to start loving you. In fact, you will find yourself loving you more than you ever have. You will start realizing that the person God created really isn't that bad. In fact, they're kind of cool. It doesn't matter what other people think of you, it's all about what you think of yourself.

It's not complicated to face your reality, but it is hard to do. Like I've said throughout this journey, prayer works. It's okay to ask God to teach you how to face your reality. However, be careful what you ask for; you might just get it. You have to be prepared for what he shows you. No, you may not like it, but you know it will be better for you in the end. Why you ask? You have already taken the first step, to be a better you. If you are sitting there reading this and taking notes, then you have already taken the first step on your journey. You made a decision, to be a better you. Now you are trying to learn a better way. You are on the right path to a new found peace.

Keep working hard, and don't give up; no matter what life throws your way. When life hand you lemons, you make lemonade and have a great time.

Facing your reality can be handled the same way. Aren't you ready to live a peaceful life? If you answered yes, it's time to start facing your reality. Peace doesn't come from mess. Peace doesn't come from chaos. Peace doesn't come from foolishness.

It's time for you to make the ultimate decision for your life. In order to have peace you have to remove and clear out the clutter in your life. If you think you have no clutter, you might want to take a closer look. I bet if you start facing your reality, you will see all the clutter amongst you. What are you waiting for? It's time to start doing some spring cleaning, winter cleaning, summer cleaning, or fall cleaning. No matter what the season may be, it's time for you to start facing your reality right now.

The Body Within

I may be physically healthy, but I am mentally weak

The medicine industry is a billion dollar industry, yet we continue to feed our body things we don't need. Six out of ten people can sit around the table and talk about medicine all day; because they have so many to take on a daily basis. We have a pill to take for every part of our body, and the question is; how many of those pills are actually working?

In today's society, we have pills for our health and our minds. Some work, but many don't. Everyone may have a different reaction to some of the medicines. Now, I am not telling you to stop taking your medicine. However, I am saying that we should be more mindful what we put in our temple. Just because the doctor prescribes it to us, doesn't mean that it will work for us.

In 2010, I was diagnosed with Lupus. I thought my life was over, and a few times it did try to take me out. However, God was not ready for me. He found favor in me, and spared my life from a disease that has no cure (so they say), and a disease that will eventually take my life. The first thing they chose to do was pump me full of medicine. Now, I am a woman who doesn't like taking medicine and full of life. However, I thought taking the medicine would save me. Boy was I wrong. The medicine was making me feel worse than I had ever felt. I was sleeping my life away, and at times felt like a zombie. I just could not seem to function. Now how can I run a business if I'm sleep all day? The pain was more severe than ever before and I was living a miserable life. I was not happy, and had to do something. I started doing my research, and got involved with other people who also suffered from Lupus. This is when I found out about other remedies and methods I could do. I started winging myself off of the medicine and started living my life again. Although I'm not a hundred percent pain free, I feel better than I was. I finally can start living my life again. I just had to find something that worked for me.

You may struggle with many things about your health, and that's okay. However, don't be a victim of your circumstances. Find what works for you. Don't just take someone's word for it. Everyone's body is different, and what may work for you may not work for me.

Your body is a temple, and we must be more mindful as to what we do to it and put in it.

1 Corinthians 3:16-17 (ESV) Know ye not that ye are the temple of God, and that the Spirit of God dwelleth in you? ... For the temple of God is holy, which temple ye are.

On this journey, it's important to be healthy physically and mentally. If you are not physically healthy, you don't have the capability of taking the first step. However, if you are not mentally healthy, you don't have the mind set to wanting to take the first step.

This journey was not an easy journey for me, especially when I first started. I wasn't physically or mentally healthy. I was all over the place. Using my illness as an excuse, as to why I couldn't take the first step. Using depression as an excuse, to say why I couldn't take the first step. The thing I love about God's grace is that he always finds favor in you, even when you don't think you're worthy.

It's time to stop making excuses, as to why you can't and start finding reasons as to why you **can**. It's time to start treating your body, as the temple God created. We must start watching what we put in our body, and who we give our body to.

Now I know sometimes we are blinded by what we want, and allow temptation to take effect. However, we have to be mindful that we can't lay down with everyone; just because they look good. When you are doing this, you are allowing your spirit to attach to someone else's and that may not be good for you. Also, there are so many diseases out there and you don't know what someone may be carrying. We have to treat out temple, as a gem. You wouldn't want to destroy your gem, so why would you want to destroy your temple? We have to be more mindful of the things we do. We are not hurting anyone else, except for ourselves.

When your mental is out of whack, your feelings and emotions tend to be all over the place. When this happens, we tend to do things out of emotions. Some people lash out when they are angry. Some people cry when they are sad. Some people go into a depression when they are confused. Our mental is a big part of our being, but at times it tends to get us into a world of trouble. As humans, we have to accept that we are emotional creatures and learn how to adapt and control our emotions. Of course that's easier said than done, but once you are aware of what you do when your emotions kick in, you will also know how to control them. Awareness is the key. A lot of time we are not aware of what we do until it's too late. On this journey you are learning to face your reality, and in doing so this will also make you aware of what you do to yourself, when your emotions kick in.

Let's start breaking it down, and giving you ways of controlling these emotions. We can't cover them all, but I will touch base on those key triggers.

Anger- I chose to start with anger first. Most of us are angry individuals, and this is when we do some of our dumbest things. Anger gets you in more trouble than just a little bit. Sometimes we find ourselves in jail, prison, dead, or brutally battered; whether it's you or someone else.

If you have an anger issue, it's time to let it go. You are not hurting anyone but you. Maybe you don't feel like you have an anger problem, but keep finding yourself in these crazy situations; the first step to recovery is acknowledgement. In order to move forward you have to acknowledge that you have an anger problem.

Here are some examples to tell you if you have an anger problem.

- Everything anyone does or says irritates you
- You are quickly to start yelling
- Clenching your jaws or gritting your teeth
- Rapid heart race
- Quick to jump and react without thinking

This is just a few things to give you a start on acknowledging if you have an anger issue. Now let's talk about some ways to control these issues when they start to occur.

If you are quickly angered by what someone says to you; you must understand that people have the right to say what they want to say. If it's not true, then why are you so angry? You have to learn how to nod, and walk away. You can't help the fact that some people don't have common sense. It's not for you to be the judge of that. You can only live your life for you and worry about you. People are going to do some things that you will not like or approve of, but remember; you don't have to associate yourself with those people. You can walk away at any time. It's a choice.

Proverbs 19:11 (ESV) Good sense makes one slow to anger, and it is his glory to overlook an offense

If you are a yeller, what are you yelling for? Getting your blood pressure all high; about to kill yourself. There is no problem worth killing yourself for. If you feel like someone is making you that angry, to point of you yelling; it's time for you to walk away. Why would you want to stay in a situation, where you constantly have to yell? Now, I realize that there are two types of yellers because some of y'all just like yelling at your children, and that's not good either. First of all, you are raising your blood pressure, and taking a chance of the kids losing their mother. Now is that something you want to do? Second, you are teaching your children that yelling is the way of life, and it's okay to be angry all the time. You're not giving your children a chance or opportunity to be their own person. The world is not full of yellers, so why must you yell. Ask yourself; is the situation really worth yelling about? Is it really worth making myself angry and taking a risk with my life? It's time to start facing your reality.

Proverbs 29:11 (ESV) A fool gives full vent to his spirit, but a wise man quietly holds it back.

If you are the clincher, please stop doing that. Again, it's still not healthy for your heart or your teeth. In reality, all you're doing is bottling that anger in and once it comes out, it's explosive. You do more damage to yourself holding in your feelings, then if you were honest and told them how you feel. You have to learn how to communicate, and understand that your feelings are important, as well. You have the right to voice your opinion and let your voice be heard. Stop bottling all that pressure up, and set it free. In order to take this journey and find your peace, you have to set it free.

Proverbs 15:1 (ESV) A soft answer turns away wrath, but a harsh word stirs up anger.

If you are the heart racer, you are surely quicker to kill yourself than anyone. This means that you could be any of the people mentioned above if not all of them. Please, take the proper steps to recovery. It doesn't matter if you have to go to counseling, or start taking this journey and find your worth. Please understand that you are worthy and valuable in this world. You wouldn't still be here if God didn't have a purpose on your life.

Romans 12:21 (ESV) Do not be overcome by evil, but overcome evil with good.

If you are the jumper, you are in a heap of trouble. You will cause ruckus any and everywhere you go. You have to learn how to think rationally before you react. This behavior makes you think everyone is against you, and you have to react to every situation when in reality you don't. Eventually you will find yourself alone. No one wants to be around someone that's always in the mix of some mess. You think trouble finds you, but in reality you are causing the trouble and you have to face your reality. It's okay to walk away from a situation. It doesn't mean that you are weak or a punk. It simply means that you are smart and adult enough to walk away from a situation, before it gets out of hand and you find yourself in a situation you will later regret.

Proverbs 15:18 (ESV) A hot-tempered man stirs up strife, but he who is slow to anger quiets contention.

Once you learn how to apply these methods to your daily routine, you will then find peace.

Depression- This is another issue that keeps us from finding our peace. Some of us are in denial of depression, but many suffer from it. This disease is not only for women. Men suffer from it as well. However, some are unaware of the signs of depression. When we are talking about being mentally healthy, we have to understand that depression plays a big part of our mental health. When they say the mind is a terrible thing to waste, they weren't lying. Without our minds, we are dead. Depression makes us feel this way, as well.

If you are not sure if you suffer from depression, here are a few symptoms to be aware of.

- Anxiety
- Mood swings
- Weight gain or loss

- Fatigue
- Restlessness
- Excessive crying
- Irritability
- Loss of interest

These are just some of the signs. When we talk about depression, there are many signs. However, just because we feel this way every now and then does not mean that we suffer from depression. It simply means that we are human. Now if you experience these symptoms more often, you are suffering from depression and should seek counseling.

Counseling isn't as bad as it may seem. For a long time, I thought counseling was only for crazy people. When I was recommended to seek counseling, I thought the person recommending it to me was just as crazy. However, I found out very quickly that I had to do something. I was spiraling extremely fast, and had to come to grips with the things going on in my life. Although, I still was leery about going to counseling, I thought maybe I should give it a try. What could it hurt? I was already losing control of me and the situation at hand. Looking for a counselor was not easy, but I was determined to find someone who could understand me. The first counselor didn't work for me, but the second counselor did. Being able to talk to someone who didn't judge me, or try to tell me what I should do was helping. By her being there, she was able to help me face some of my realities. Going to her for a year, I noticed I was feeling better and had a better outlook on life. Once that happened, I stopped my sessions. Who would've known, that years down the road I would find myself back in therapy? Of course, we would like to think that we will be great and nothing will happen to us ever again. How wrong was I?

Unfortunately, life doesn't work that way. The second time I found myself in therapy was much worse than the first time. I said that to say, "Never stop going because you start feeling a little better. You might find yourself in a worse situation."

Never think you are alone or the only one who suffers from depression. Depression is a severe disease, and it doesn't matter how others look at it. However, you have the strength to overcome and control your depression.

Psalm 34:17 (KJV) The righteous cry out, and the Lord hears them; he delivers them from all their troubles.

No matter how much we cry, God hears all of our cries. You are never alone. Although you may feel as if the world is against you, and you have no purpose in life; God has a purpose on all of our lives. Man will not love you unconditionally, but God's love is always unconditional. It never changes no matter what the circumstance may be. When you start feeling unloved and unworthy, you must hold on to God's love.

1 Peter 5:6-7 tells us to humble ourselves under God's mighty hand that he may lift you up in due time. Cast all your anxiety on him because he cares for you.

Once we realize God's love for us, we will start loving ourselves and find a way to fight depression. If you are uncertain on how to fight depression, here are a few tips.

- **Reach out and stay connected**- When we are depressed, the mind tells us to withdraw and go into hibernation. This is never good. If you do as such, it will be even harder for you to break the depression cycle. Reaching out to friends and family, can be exactly what you need to break your depression and stay connected. You don't have to be ashamed of your situation. Everyone makes mistakes, or hurt from nasty breakups, divorce, death, etc. Having a great support team will help you to get through these things; even when you feel they are unbearable.

Here a few examples on how to reach out and get the support you need.

- Look for people who make you feel safe and cared for without judgment.
- Phone calls and video chatting
- Keep up with social activities; even if you don't feel like it.
- Support others
- Care for a pet
- Join a support group

These tips should help you stay connected to those you care about and fight the depression cycle. If that doesn't help, try this next method.

- **Do things that make you feel good**- I know right now you are asking yourself; how are you supposed to do the things that make you feel good when you are not in the mood and just don't feel like it?

In order to overcome depression, you must do the things that will relax your mind and remember why life is so important to you. Although, you may not want to do these things at the time, by forcing yourself to do your daily activities you may realize that this is what helped you to manage your stress in the first place and knock you out of that depression. I know for me, I find myself writing, working, or taking a long walk to ease my stress levels. These are some of the things I enjoy doing, and why I throw myself into the things I love to do, I tend to forget that I was depressed, or why I was depressed at the time. What works for me may not work for you. If you are not sure what you love to do, here is your chance to start exploring and finding you. You can never beat depression if you don't know what you like or love to do.

If you are not sure as to what you like to do, here is a general list to get you started.

- Movies
- Breakfast, Lunch, or Dinner with a friend or loved one
- Visit a museum
- Write
- Go for a walk
- Workout with a friend or loved one
- Schedule weekly date night with friends or loved one
- Volunteer
- Have a small get together with friends
- Game night
- Fishing
- Concert or Comedy show

Although there are many things you can do, these are just a few to get you started. Find what works for you. Listening to music could be one, but when we are depressed we tend to listen to the saddest music we can find. I would suggest you stay away from music unless it's upbeat and give you power and the encouragement you need.

- **Develop a wellness toolbox**- Now I know you're trying to figure out what this is, but everyone needs one. A wellness toolbox is a list of things you can do, to keep your depression in check.

Although you may be having a hard time keeping your depression in check, here are a few items you can add to your wellness toolbox.

- **Aim for eight hours of sleep**- Although this may be difficult to do, especially if you suffer from insomnia; it is something we have to aim for. When you don't get enough sleep, you tend to suffer from mood swings and lack of energy which can cause depression. Of course sleeping too much is a sign of depression as well. You must find a healthy sleep balance. If you suffer from insomnia; speak with your doctor and find out what you can do to treat this.
- **Find ways to keep your stress in check**- Life is stressful, but in your life you must find out what is stressing you, and eliminate those stress factors. If you're not sure what is stressing you out, start with some of these key factors: work, money, unhealthy relationships, or children. Remember...why stress over the things you can't change?
- **Practice relaxation techniques**- Breathing, meditation, and yoga are just a few things you can do to practice relaxation. By doing these

simple things on a daily basis, will help you to relieve the tension, regain control, and kick depression straight in the ass.

Although these are the main things that should be in your wellness toolbox, here are a few more things you can add for a quick mood boost.

- List all the things you like about yourself
- Read a good book
- Watch a funny movie or TV show
- Take a long hot bath
- Do something spontaneous
- Take care of things on your "to do" list

Now this next tip may blow you away, but it's also an important aspect when it comes to depression. When we are talking about being healthy, you can't forget to do this next tip.

- **Eat healthy**- Remember when your grandmother used to tell you, "You are what you eat?" Well this is true. Certain foods we put in our body affects the way our brain functions. You have to be mindful of your food intake and the risk you take.

Although you may eat healthy, it's important that you don't skip meals and minimize your sugar and carbs. Like most people, when you don't eat you tend to have less energy and may tend to feel irritated.

You may be like me and love sweets, but when you overdo it, you tend to crash hard after coming down off that sugar high. Although cakes and pies are "feel good" foods, they are not good for you. So find another way to suffice the cake and pies. It's okay to substitute them for fruits.

I truly hope these few tips help you to fight depression and live a healthier, peaceful life. If none of these tips work for you, I highly suggest you seek counseling as soon as possible.

Illness- Many of us deal with some type of illness that we can't control. Now we talked about it a little bit earlier, but that was on the medicine side and what we put in our bodies. In this segment we will cover ways on how to overcome our illnesses.

So many times, we speak on our illness. Some use their illness as a crutch, as to why they can't live their purpose. You can continue to tell yourself how sick you are, or you can speak health and life over your body. We tend to forget that the tongue is a mighty sword, and the things we speak into the atmosphere will come to past.

Proverbs 12:18 (ESV) There is one whose rash words are like sword thrusts, but the tongue of the wise brings healing.

Being sick is not what we want to be, but it tends to be a way of life when you have no control over your illness. Suffering with Lupus on a daily basis is extremely hard, and I tend to go on an emotional rollercoaster with it. However, I have found a few ways to not allow it to control me and take over my life. Although I can't control it, I have found ways to endure it.

I remember when I was diagnosed with Lupus. I felt like life was over for me. I felt like no one would ever understand or love me with this condition. I felt hopeless, and worthless. What was I supposed to do with a disease I can't control and a disease without a cure? Yeah, I could've gave up right then and there, and trust me; I wanted to. However, God didn't want me to give up on life, or me; I had to fight through the pain, and know he would carry me through. No matter how difficult it is to get out of bed, you have to fight. Don't allow the sickness to take over.

Here are a few helpful tips that helped me to get through the pain.

- **Be open to treatments that doctors won't tell you about**- There are other methods, other than taking medicines, which can help you get through the pain. Find those methods, do your research, and don't be afraid to try them. You never know what may work for you.
- **Surround yourself with people who support you**- If you are surrounded by people who don't understand or support you through these trying times it's okay to cut off these relationships. Although it may be hard to do, it's a must because being in these unhealthy relationships can cause your health to deteriate even quicker.
- **Don't compare your journey to others**- Comparing your journey to someone else's journey can be detrimental to your health, and make you over think it. Their journey may not be the same as yours, although you suffer with the same illness. If it can't help you in a positive way, then don't compare your journey.
- **Be your own advocate**- Nobody cares about your health more than you. Don't allow doctors or people to tell you anything. Find out for

yourself, and fight for the proper treatment. People may doubt you, but who knows your body better than you?

- **Find something you love to do**- When you love what you do, you don't have time to think about your illness. When you have a hobby, your mind is occupied and your soul is full of joy.
- **Find ways to laugh and smile every day**- Laughter is the key to happiness. If you are talking about the pain or your illness all day, you will find yourself in the dumps. However, if you are enjoying life and finding ways to make you happy; you can overcome the pain you feel on a daily basis, even if you are confined to the bed at the moment.
- **Love yourself**- Love you, no matter what your body is telling you. You are worthy to be loved, and are capable of doing anything you set your mind to. Don't be a victim of your illness, just because you can't do what you used to do. Sometimes, God has to slow us down in order for us to make a change.
- **Don't become your illness**- Its okay to be the voice or an advocate for your illness, but don't allow it to control your life. Just because you are sick does not mean that you have to be your illness. The world is lucky to have you, if you push the issue too much you may find yourself retracting.
- **Be patient**- Healing doesn't happen overnight, and the older you get the longer it takes to heal.

You didn't get sick overnight, so don't expect to heal overnight. What you may have may never heal, and that's something you will always have to live with. However, you don't have to become obsessed with your illness and feel as if your life is over. Your life is not over until God is ready for you. So be patient and live your life to the fullest.

You may not look like you feel, and some people will always treat you as if nothing is wrong with you; and that's okay, you must not allow that to bother you when they have never walked a day in your shoes.

When people look at me, they never think I suffer from Lupus, but there are days I can't get out of my bed and sometimes I have blackouts. How would one know these things about me just by looking at me? They wouldn't, but it's easy to judge a person based on looks alone.

Never judge a book by its cover. You never know what the insides may hold.

By applying these few tips on a daily basis, you will find yourself being healthier within; physically, mentally, and emotionally.

Being Able to Say "NO"

No means no...it's not the new yes

Why is it so hard to say no, and actually mean it? Could it be because the people in our lives tend to make us feel guilty at times?

When we say no, we have to stick to our guns and mean what we say. Don't allow others to make you feel guilty for telling them no. It's okay to say no sometimes. When you say no, it does not mean that you are being mean or selfish. It can simply mean that you are not able to do it, or don't have the means to do the things that's being asked of you. It could also mean that you just simply don't want to do it and that's okay too.

You must remember that you're not obligated to anyone but you and yours. In this chapter we will discuss being able to say no to family, friends, and loved ones; and be okay with it.

Matthew 5:37 (ESV) Let what you say be simply 'Yes' or 'No'; anything more than this comes from evil.

When you are indecisive you leave room for someone to change your mind, even when you really can't or don't want to. When you do this, you are being dishonest with yourself and others, as well.

Saying "No" to your friends- Do you ever find yourself finding it hard to say "No" to your friends? Is it because you feel that if you say no, you may lose a friend? Maybe, you feel as if you will be a bad friend if you say no.

Many of us have felt this way so many times. What I have learned over the years is that your true friends will understand if you say no. They will not walk away, or have an attitude because you said no; unless, you are the friend that is always in need, but when they need you; you are unable to come through for them.

Now if you're the friend who is always giving and giving, you're probably wondering, when is it okay to say no when you're all your friend has.

Anytime is okay to say "NO". You may be all your friend has, but you also have to ask yourself, if it's hurting you or helping you. We are supposed to be there for our friends, but we are not supposed to allow our friends to take our kindness for weakness. You have to stand your ground sometimes, even when you can help them. This method is not being rude, or selfish, but by doing things this way; you are showing your friend that they can rely on you, but not all the time. If you are willing to do everything for them, than how can they be self-sufficient?

When we call ourselves adults, we must live by the law of the land; self preservation. Now some may make this harder than what it really is, but you can't call yourself an adult and refuse to take care of your responsibilities. The world owes you nothing, but you owe it all to yourself to be reliant on you. Now if this applies to you, don't you think it applies to your friends?

Right now, time is of the essence and we have no time to waste waiting for others to get their minds right and decide what they want out of life. People are only to be in our lives for a sec, a season, or a lifetime. You have to figure out how long the people who cross your path are supposed to be in your circle.

Remember, friends will not allow you to foot the tab all the time, and think its okay. Friends will not take your kindness for weakness, because they know you will give them your last. Be mindful of what you are willing to put in your spirit, because we are who we hang around. The meaning birds of a feather flock together is so true. If you are hanging with people who smoke and drink all day, then you are bound to do the same thing. If you are hanging in the streets with people slanging drugs all day, then you are most likely doing the same thing.

True friends know how to give, as well as receive. True friends will not allow you to give your last and go in the hole for them, no matter what their situation may be. True friends will also pay you back and make sure you're both going to win. So if you can't say "NO" or scared to say "NO" to your friends; they are not your friend(s), and its okay to break away from these unhealthy relationships. If you shall stay, you will find yourself in a world of trouble, and peace is not on the radar anywhere.

Saying "No" to your family- Now saying no to your family can be a little trickier. However, they are no exception to the rule.

Family knows how to touch those spots, to make you feel guilty, but don't get caught up in their tangled web.

The other day, I had someone ask, "How do you say no to your parents when they gave you life?"

It's never easy to say no to those who gave you life. However, it's okay for you to say no to them as well; although, they gave you life. When you were a child your parents didn't always say yes to you. They had to tell you no to some things in order for you to understand that it was okay to say no. Now if it was easy for them to say no to you, don't you think the same should apply to you? You don't have to say no all the time, because they will be there for you when no one else is, but if you have parents who haven't been in your life like that; don't get caught up in your feelings. Feeling that if you say no, they will not love you, and the relationship you are trying to build will be destroyed. Remember...parents don't mooch off their children. If anything, they want to see you grow and be a better person. Now I realize every situation is different, and you have to handle your decision accordingly.

If you are having a hard time saying no to your siblings, you have to let that go. It's okay to be your brother/sister's keeper, but you also have to be mindful. If you think your brother or sister won't play you; you are sadly mistaken. Although I love my brothers and sisters, and will do anything for them; I also have to be mindful. I can't allow their lives and situations to affect my life. If I am able to help them without hurting myself, then I will do it. However, I am not going to help them with something so irrelevant; ex. Partying, drinking, smoking, shopping.

In some cases, you have to treat your siblings as if they are your friends; especially, when it comes to saying no.

Now, this next section I must say is by far the hardest.

Saying "No", to your spouse/mate- As a spouse, I find it very difficult to say no to my husband, but find that he has it easy saying **no** to me. If this sounds like you and your spouse, it's time to reevaluate the situation. As women, we feel our jobs are to nurture and take care of our family; no matter the circumstances. We have been known to go in debt behind our spouse(s), as well. I know I am guilty of this. I have done a lot of dumb things, to make sure my spouse is happy. However, over the years I have come to realize that no matter how much you give or what you do, they will never be satisfied and it's not going to make them love you any more than they already do.

Every time my husband asked me something, I found myself saying yes, or breaking my neck to do what he wanted me to do. It didn't matter what the consequences were, I made sure to do whatever he asked of me. Boy how quickly did I find out that the more I said yes, the more he was taking my love and kindness for granted, and the further I was finding myself in debt. Now, I know you're asking yourself; where is the peace in that? There isn't any, but I will share with you on how I was able to say no to my spouse, and not feel guilty. Now trust me when I say, it was not easy but something that needed to be done.

After being his "yes woman" for so many years, it finally felt good to stand up and say no. It wasn't easy the first time I said no, but every time after that I found it becoming a little bit easier. For me, saying no was not the hard part. It was the guilt that I had to endure after I said no. I felt guilty because that was my husband I was saying no to, and of course the guilt he laid on me didn't make it any easier.

Although he was making me feel guilty about saying no to him, I had to find my strength and voice. This is when **prayer** has to be your number one source. Without prayer, I was not able to say no to him and I kept finding myself digging a deeper hole for me. A hole that he was not going to pull me out of, a hole he was going to bury me in. I know some of you know exactly what I mean. When we are in financial debt, we feel as if we are being buried and may never see daylight.

Once I started saying no to my husband, I found myself slowly but surely being able to rise up out of that hole; he was trying to bury me in. As a spouse, you have to find your strength in God and rise above your circumstances. It doesn't matter if you are a husband or a wife, at some point we have to start thinking about our future. Marriage is about longevity and commitment. You can never do any of that if one is busy taking and the other is busy giving. At some point in your marriage, you have to ask yourself, are we saving for the long haul? Do we have something to fall back on? Are we building the life God wants us to have? If you answered those anything but with a yes, it's time to reevaluate your situation and maybe even your marriage. No I'm not telling you to leave your marriage, but I am saying that you have to reevaluate the situation within your marriage. Two people should be on the same path, trying to go in the same direction. Marriage can't work if you're going in different directions. It's okay to be your own person, but remember...when two are joined together, they become one.

Ecclesiastes 4:9 (ESV) Two are better than one, because they have a good reward for their toil.

When you join together, and become one accord you will be able to do great things, and see yourself being in a stable place and living life abundantly together.

No one ever said marriage would be easy, but it's a choice and you have to work hard in it; even if you have to say "**No**" sometimes. Just make sure that when you're saying no, it's not to be spiteful. You have to say no for your better good.

Now if you are just building your relationship and you see some things you don't quite agree with, it's okay to say no. Stick to your grounds and allow the person to understand what you will and will not accept. See, if you started making better decisions in the dating process and being honest with ourselves and our mates, it would eliminate a lot of divorces.

If you are always saying yes during the dating process, don't expect to say no during the marriage process. It doesn't work like that. Remember...whatever you start in the beginning you have to continue until the very end.

Make your no's a strong no, and your yes a yes. Don't be indecisive as to what you want. This could lead to confusion and guilt in the end. When people see a way in, they will use it. So be mindful of what you say, and sturdy on how you say things.

Saying "No" to your children- Allow me to put this disclaimer in here right now. **This section may make a lot of you feel a certain type of way. However, this book is about growth and finding your new found peace. It's time to face your reality.**

Now that we have gotten that out of the way, don't be alarmed by the things you are about to read. This is more for my Queens. However fellas please don't think you get away scot free.

As mothers, our jobs are to nurture and protect our children. However, some of us take it way too far. We have to remember that our children are our children; not our mates, or our friends.

Some of us are so busy wanting to be our children's friend that we forget its okay to say no. When you refuse to say no to your child, what are you teaching them exactly?

Proverbs 22:6 (ESV) Train up a child in the way he should go; even when he is old, he will not depart from it.

Refusing to say no, you are teaching your child that they are entitled. The reality of it is; they're not. If you're teaching them these things now, it will be much worse when they are adults. They will feel as if the whole world owes them something, and you and I both know; nothing in this life is free. Not even air.

You don't have to buy, or cater to their every need. It's not mandatory that they have every pair of new Jordan's that hit the shelf, or every pair of $400 jeans. As long as they have clothes on their back and shoes on their feet, that is all that matters. You shouldn't have to go into debt, to keep up with the Jones's or show your children that you love them. Keeping a roof over their heads, and spending time with them should be a great way of showing them that you love them.

We have to start teaching our children the value of money, or they will always feel as if it's to spend however. They will never understand paying bills, or taking care of themselves when they become adults if you continue to spoil and cater to their every need. You are the parent and they are the child. You gave them life, and it's okay to say no. If you start off saying no when they are babies, then by the time they are teenagers they will respect the word "**no**" a lot better.

Proverbs 13:24 (ESV) Whoever spares the rod hates his son, but he who loves him is diligent to discipline him.

Discipline does not mean beating your child, but being able to say no and stand on it. They have to understand that they can't have everything they want, or everything they see.

If you can't find a way to say no to your children, how will you be able to find your new found peace when you are busy taking care of children that will never leave the nest?

Start saying no at an early age, and life will be better for you once they are grown. You don't want to have grown kids who keep calling on mama to cook, clean, and provide for them financially. If you make it easy for them to come to you all the time, they will never try. You have to show them how to be independent and stand on their own. This is our jobs as parents, but mother's especially.

Now fathers, some of you are absent in their lives and need to do better by your children. If you are not their on a regular and they call and say they need something, it's not your job to say no all the time. If you are busy always saying no, or that you can't; how do you expect them to be towards you, or in this society? Don't lie to your children with that "we'll see" bull crap either. It's easier to say no, then to lie to them. Children or not dumb by far, and you have to stop treating them as such.

Now for the fathers in their children's lives on a regular, please be mindful of how you say no. You don't have to be aggressive when you say no, or sarcastic. A simple no, and go on about your business will do. However, always make your no stern, so that they will understand where you're coming from.

I know raising children is not an easy task, and there isn't a handbook in the world that can tell us about our children. Only life and time can reveal what our next move should be with our children. However, in order to find your new found peace you must be able to say no to your children. It will only hurt for a little while, but in the end you will be glad that you did. Your no just might save your child's life.

Coping with Financial Delays

My money may be short, but it won't determine how I live my life

You may not have enough money, but that doesn't mean that your life has to end or stop. It just simply means you have to adjust according to your finances.

Often times we find ourselves in a greater debt than we ever imagined, and most of the times it's because we mismanage our finances and I use that term lightly.

So many of us are so busy trying to fit in with society and live like the Jones's, that we forget our money isn't long enough to do either.

In this chapter you will learn new ways to get a grip on your finances, and how to cope with those financial delays; when you have more bills than money.

I understand how depressing financial stability can be, but I'm here to share with you ways that I cope, and how to get through those depressing times.

Hebrews 13:5 (ESV) Keep your life free from love of money, and be content with what you have, for he has said, "I will never leave you nor forsake you."

I live by this verse right here. Once you understand that no matter what you go through God will always be there, you will find your new found peace.

Now don't get me wrong, I like money; but I'm not in love with money. I understand that you must have money to live, but I also understand that God said if I have faith in him, he will supply all my needs. So I don't worry if I have money or not. When I am broke and need something, God always shows up right on time and provides my needs.

Often times, we get so caught up in having money that we are willing to go through any extent to get it or have it.

Matthew 6:24 (ESV) No one can serve two masters, for either he will hate the one and love the other, or he will be devoted to the one and despise the other. You cannot serve God and money.

As some point in our lives, we have to determine who we are going to serve. For me and my house, we will continue to serve God and know that he will provide all of our needs. So you see I am content with what God has provided for me. I live accordingly to my money; not by the Jones's, society, or the neighbors down the street. I am not here to please others, or to be seen, but to do the work of God.

Proverbs 13:16 (ESV) In everything the prudent acts with knowledge, but a fool flaunts his folly.

Now, you have to ask yourself who are you. You don't have to flaunt, or live above your means to be seen or noticed. As long as God notices who you are, you are important. Having the best car, the best house, or lots of money don't make you anything but a person with material things. Can any of that give you peace, Integrity, or Perseverance? You probably thought about this long and hard, and some of you are probably still thinking about this. However, if you think that these things can do that for you, I need you to understand it's only temporary. Meaning...it will only make you feel good for a moment.

When we talk about finding our new found peace, we are talking about for a lifetime; not just a moment.

So many times, we do things for the moment. We never stop and think about the rest of our lives, or our futures.

I know you're probably thinking that you don't make enough to save any money, or you don't have enough to think about your future, but I'm here to prove you wrong. If you sit and calculate all the money you spend doing dumb stuff, you will probably have a nice little savings. Now just think if you took half of that and put away how much you will have.

We often feel as if we need a lot to be able to save something, but in reality we don't. Just think, if you took five dollars from each pay check and put away, you would have 60 dollars (if you get paid monthly), 120 dollars (if you get paid bi-weekly), and 240 dollars (if you get paid weekly). Now this is what you will have saved for the year. It may not seem like a lot, but just think what you will have in five or ten years. No it may not be enough to buy a house, or buy a brand new car outright. However, it's enough for a down payment or that exotic vacation you've been dreaming about. It only takes a little bit to get you started. Now if you can put more back, by all means do so. You are building a nest egg for your future, and don't allow anyone to tell you what is or isn't enough. Remember...you don't have to be rich to be happy. We were born to be at peace and to be happy, but somehow we always find a way to stand in our own way. Once we decide to move out of our own way, we will start seeing a big difference in our attitudes, our homes, our children, and our financial situations. The choice is yours. Don't allow bad decisions, or listening to others who mean you no good cause you financial delays, or delays to your new found peace.

You only have one life to life, so why should you allow what others have to say affect the way you live your life? Live your life to the fullest, but within your means. Anything other than that is uncivilized, and peace is not in your cards. This is definitely something for you to think about.

Figure out where you want to be and strive to be the best. You can do anything you put your mind to, and find your new found peace within your budget.

Relate, Release, Rebuild

In order to get past the pain you have to relate to the pain, release the pain, and rebuild yourself again

When you saw the title of this chapter how did it make you feel?

Now think about that for a little while. In this section, you may be filled with unresolved emotions, but this is the time to let it go.

No one said life would be easy, but it's what you do with it that makes life so great. During this chapter be honest with yourself, take notes, and come to a resolution. No it's never easy facing our reality, but since you have been doing it throughout this entire process; it should be a piece of cake to you. However, I know this is really when the challenge kicks in and we start lying to ourselves. Pretending we don't feel like that, or pretending to be something we're really not.

This is your time to make a solid decision about your life, but don't keep playing yourself. You see, it's easy to do as such; I have done it many times. Well, that was until the day I chose to stop playing and lying to myself. I had to understand that I wasn't hurting anyone but myself, and it was me who was getting the short end of the stick.

Once I got tired of my own foolishness, and standing in my way; I knew it was time to truly do something about it. Although I was afraid of what may happen or what people would feel, I had to understand that I was doing this for me. See, the problem with most of us is; we are so busy trying to change someone else to fit into our lives, when we don't even know how to fit into our own lives. Instead of concentrating on changing someone else, we need to concentrate on changing ourselves.

The world would be a much better place if we worried about ourselves, and how to make ourselves better. We have to understand that people who are not ready to change won't, and those who are will. It doesn't matter what you do or say; nothing can make a person do something they are not ready to do.

During this process, our goal is to work on ourselves; not everyone else. Our goal is to find our peace, but how can we do that when we are so busy giving it away to those who don't deserve it?

During this chapter, we will hit some key pointers and factors on how to concentrate on you and find your new found peace. You will learn how to face your circumstances head on, and make them better for you.

Relate- In order to make your circumstances better, you first have to relate to them.

Through this process you have learned how to face your reality, so relating to your circumstances should be a breeze; unless, you're still lying to yourself. At this point, I hope you are past that point.

Take your time to determine the circumstances in your life that is causing you a problem. Once you have recognized it/or them, start relating to them one by one. **Do not** try to take them all on at once. If you do, you will find yourself worse off than when you first started the process.

Now that you know what is holding you back or keeping you from your new found peace, let's dissect them one by one. You have acknowledged the problem(s), now you must relate to them. Meaning...what caused this? Why do you feel this way? How did you allow it to get this far?

As you're asking yourself these questions, I know you're saying to yourself that this is harder than you thought. Of course it is, because facing your reality is always hard; no matter how long you've been doing it. Till this day, I still have trouble facing my reality, but I do and feel better when I do.

Answering these few questions may have made you realize some things about yourself that you may not like, or wonder how in the world did I get myself into this situation; especially when I know this is not me. In life, we do some stupid things. But instead of punishing yourself, or beating yourself up you have to look at it as a lesson. Without the lessons of life, how can we grow? How can we become stronger than before? During this journey, you should be taking each step as a lesson. And this is no different.

Release- Now that you have related to your circumstances, it's time to release.

So many times we hold on to the things we can't change, or things we can't control. Why do we hold on to things that hurt us, or tear us apart? I will tell you why. Most of the time, it's out of fear. We hold on because we are scared of the outcome. When in reality, if we did let go we would be in a better position. The pain we tend to feel is caused by ourselves, and the more we wallow in it; the worse we feel. At some point, we have to decide if it's worth it or not and I'm here to tell you right now; nothing is ever worth giving up your happiness, or your peace.

Proverbs 3:5-6 (ESV) - Trust in the LORD with all your heart, and do not lean on your own understanding. In all your ways acknowledge him, and he will make straight your paths.

Once we trust in God, we can release any and everything that is not of him. We don't have to understand it, or make any sense of it. As long as we are at peace, why would you want to analyze the situation? Take it at face value, and accept it for what it is and let it go. It shouldn't matter if it's a relationship, job, friendship, marriage, or personal.

When we refuse to release the things we can't change, we continue to hold ourselves in bondage. Now how do you expect to find peace when you're living a life of bondage within yourself?

Matthew 11:28 (ESV) - Come to me, all who labor and are heavy laden, and I will give you rest.

So if God will give you rest, why do we continue to block it with our own foolishness, and selfishness? I know you're probably saying that you are not selfish, but you have to really face your reality and look at your life for what it is. A lot of the decisions we make, is for our own selfishness. We know it's not right, but something inside of us says; go ahead, take a chance, everything will be okay. Does this sound familiar? I know that I have done this so many times to myself, and afterwards wanted to kick myself in the butt. However, instead of wallowing and punishing myself for the decisions I chose to make I decided to figure out what I needed to do to fix my situation and get myself out of it. Instead of retaliating or making the situation any worse than what it was, I chose to relate, release, and rebuild. It wasn't easy, but worth taking a chance.

Rebuild- You have related to your situation, and released the things you can't control; now it's time to rebuild.

When you are rebuilding, it means you have to take one brick at a time and make sure it's secure. If you realized that one of the things keeping you in bondage was a broken relationship, I hope you pinpointed the problem and released the pain and hurt you were holding on to so that you can rebuild it; if you decide to. Now if you have chosen not to fix a relationship with someone, I hope you made the decision because it is the best thing for you.

Now, if you are holding on to a relationship that you need to let go, I'm telling you not to go backwards. Ask yourself if you're holding on because of fear, or because you are being selfish.

Proverbs 27:6 (ESV) – Faithful are the wounds of a friend; profuse are the kisses of an enemy.

Friendship- If you and a friend fell out over something petty and ridiculous, it's necessary to rebuild that friendship. Real friends come once in a lifetime, and there's not many of them out there. Friends are your brothers and sisters. Yes you may fight, but in the end you still love one another.

Now if that friend has done something so bad that it's caused you not to trust them; you definitely want to ask yourself if it's worth rebuilding.

Trust is given, and always hard to get back once broken. If it was that bad and you know that you may never be able to trust them, don't try to make something that will never be. You should never have to be in doubt, or uncomfortable with the company you keep.

Friendships are made to last a lifetime, no matter what you go through. However, don't be deceived by those who mean you no good.

Relationships- This section will cover a few things, because I want to make sure you are clear on what to rebuild and what to release and why.

Family- Many times we want to hold a grudge against our family, but we have to understand that we can't choose our family.

The majority of the time its family who hurts us the most. This doesn't mean the relationship can't be rebuilt, but it also don't mean; you can't release the relationship(s).

I know sometimes family try to make us feel that we can't let them go because we're family, but there is nothing that says we have to keep fooling with them. It doesn't change that they are family, it only change on how you handle them.

Remember...you only get one family and if the relationship is worth rebuilding than do so. If it isn't, don't continue to hold on to something that will keep you angry and in hurt every time you see them. Family or no family, they are not worth giving up your peace.

Significant other- Relationships are never easy when it's dealing with someone else's flaws, ways, and attitude.

Back in the day, the women used to say; it's better to have a piece of a man, than to have no man at all. The sad thing is, for many years many women have lived by this rule. We have taken much abuse, and lived with some things that we didn't like. A lot of times, we are so comfortable with accepting having a piece of man that we are willing to go back and try to rebuild something that can never be fixed. We do these things all because we don't want to have no man at all.

Now of course we do some crazy things to good men and this will cause the relationship to be shaky. If you realized that your attitude and demeanor is running off a great man; you need to rebuild it a.s.a.p. If your pride is too high, and you're waiting on him to come to you; keep waiting. There is always someone out there waiting on him to cross her path, and when he does; the only thought of you will be what you left behind. When a man truly loves you, he is willing to put up with your good and bad and all he wants is for you to do the same.

No relationship is perfect, and it does take some work. If it's worth rebuilding, by all means do so. If you left or they left for bigger reasons, don't go backwards. Letting go was the best thing you could've done for each other.

Now men if you know you did her wrong, and she needed to walk out on you; don't be mad. Accept what you did wrong and acknowledge it and make a commitment to not do it again. Don't ask for her forgiveness, if you're not ready to change your ways.

However, it's not cool to take any abuse or mistreatment if you're doing everything you can to build your relationship and treat her like the Queen she is. You deserve to have peace and know that you're worthy to be loved. If you know she's not going to change, don't put yourself into a deeper situation by going backwards.

Evaluate every situation and make sure it's worth rebuilding before you just dive in head first. Don't make the same dumb decision twice; which we tend to do sometimes when we are in our feelings or under distress.

If you are not sure as to what decision to make, always take it to God first, and be patient for your answer. If you listen, you will find your answer to rebuilding any relationship and your life.

Marriage – I saved marriage for last, because it's a lot more complicated than most think.

When you get married, you become one. You are equally yoked. However, when you are doing it for selfish reasons it's hard to say you are equally yoked. At that point, we find ourselves going in opposite directions and living miserable lives. One may feel like things are great, while the other is finding ways to fulfill the void left behind. This then causes lies and deceit. However, you are married and most rather live a lie than to leave a broken marriage.

For a long time, I was that lady. I married for love, he married for stability. As I was trying to build our marriage, he was trying to fulfill a void that I could never fulfill; no matter what I did, or how hard I tried.

I was ready for marriage and willing to do whatever it took for my marriage. However, he wasn't ready for marriage. Not because I didn't love him, but because I wasn't the woman he really wanted to marry.

Now don't think that I came to that conclusion over night. It took me a very long time to realize this. I had to take these steps throughout this journey you're on right now to realize what it really was, and take it at face value. Do you think that I wanted to admit that my husband didn't really love me because he's always been in love with someone else? Not only is he in love with someone else that he doesn't want to admit to, but he doesn't truly love himself; so, how could he ever love me? No, it wasn't easy, but I had to face my reality.

Instead of punishing myself or wallowing in my pity, I decided to relate to the situation. Once I gave it to God and asked him for insight, he allowed me to see what I did wrong and what I could do better. I then released the hurt and pain I was holding on to, and started remembering why I married him in the first place. I felt as if it was worth rebuilding, when in reality I knew it wasn't. My selfishness and fear of being punished by God for not giving my marriage a chance made me go back and work it out; although deep down in my heart, I knew it was a mistake. Instead of me listening to God and taking heed of the message he gave me; I chose to do what I wanted to do. Over time, I realized that rebuilding was not what he wanted. He really wanted out, but I came back and made it easy for him to do what he wanted to do.

My story may sound familiar, and you have asked yourself a million times; why do you stay? The answer to that is...love and being a good wife/husband. When you value the vows you took, the last thing you want to do is feel as if you haven't done everything in your power to make it work.

Rebuilding your marriage is never easy, but we also have to remember that it takes two to rebuild a marriage; not one. Both parties have to be on the same page and willing to walk in the same direction. When you say "I do" you take on a big responsibility. Not only are you responsible for you, but you are responsible for them. However, it's not your job to change your mate into something you want them to be. You married them for a reason, and if you can't love them for them; don't get married.

We have to remember that love doesn't hurt. Love is gentle and pure. I know you're probably ready to fight me on this, but I say that because; how can love hurt when God's love is gentle and pure? Marriage should be the same. We will have our ups and downs, but we will fight through the good and bad. Yes, sometimes you feel like you want to strangle your mate; but it's always something they will do to make you realize why you love them so much.

If you're at this point within your marriage, it's definitely worth working on and rebuilding.

If you're in an abusive marriage, I would not suggest you stay or try to rebuild something that will not get any better; it doesn't matter if you are a wife or a husband. Abuse is abuse, and no one deserves to be abused or mistreated. God gave us each other to love, cherish, and comfort one another; no matter what storm we may face. He didn't put us on this earth to abuse and mistreat each other. We must do better and start treating one another as the Kings and Queens we truly are.

Ephesians 5:22-33 (ESV) - Wives, submit to your own husbands, as to the Lord. For the husband is the head of the wife even as Christ is the head of the church, his body, and is himself its Savior. Now as the church submits to Christ, so also wives should submit in everything to their husbands. Husbands love your wives, as Christ loved the church and gave himself up for her, that he might sanctify her, having cleansed her by the washing of water with the word, so that he might present the church to himself in splendor, without spot or wrinkle or any such thing, that she might be holy and without blemish. In the same way husbands should love their wives as their own bodies. He who loves his wife loves himself. For no one ever hated his own flesh, but nourishes and cherishes it, just as Christ does the church...

If you're not ready to give your all, then don't give anything at all. Walking on the fence can get you severely hurt; all because you're not ready to be honest with yourself or your spouse.

If none of these things apply to you, it's your time to start rebuilding yourself. You have related to the things causing your grief, heartache and problems. You have released the things keeping you in bondage and now it's time to rebuild you.

It's time to reclaim your life and do what you have to do to start living your life abundantly and having the peace you deserve.

It will take some time to rebuild you, but it will be well worth it in the end. Remember...your peace is worth more than anything in the world.

Rebranding Your Life...Finding your inner peace

Finding your inner peace is something you have to hold
on to.
The world can't give you the peace God can; so why
keep giving your peace to man?

You have finally made it to the last section of this
process. Along this journey you have found out a lot of things
about yourself. If you focused on anyone other than you, I
would suggest you start all over. You can't find your peace if
you're concentrating on someone other than you.

Throughout this journey you have taken so much in and
gained many tools. Now it's time to put all the tools you gained
together, and start making it happen.

At this point, you should have a clearer heart and mind.
When we talk about rebranding ourselves, it means changing
the way we think and react to situations that's not really
complicated or serious. In fact, some of the things we deal with
throughout our lives don't even belong to us. It's always

someone else's problem. When situations like this occur, it's okay to say no or simply move on. Don't continue to give away your peace; especially, now that you are starting to find it within yourself.

Also, don't be afraid to set boundaries. Setting boundaries doesn't mean you're acting funny. It simply means that you are refusing to allow others to steal your peace. What others may call acting funny, you have to see it as protecting your peace. As for me, I will protect my peace at all cost.

Going through this same journey made me realize a lot about myself, but it also taught me how to think. If I'm always thinking negative, of course I'm going to get a negative reaction. However, if I think positively and logically I will get better results. This is all a part of rebranding.

In order to find your inner peace, you must be at peace mentally, physically, and spiritually. They go hand in hand. You can't have one without the other.

If you're feeling more at ease mentally, physically, and spiritually than you have followed the steps like you were supposed to and now it's time to start re-branding your life.

Start putting all of your goals in motion and know that you can do all things through Christ whom strengthens you. You are not allowing the world to dictate your life. God gave you a purpose and now it's time to live your purpose. You may be using your age as an excuse as to why you feel like it's too late to live your purpose. I'm here to tell you, to stop making excuses. It' better to try late in life than to never try at all and wonder why you didn't, or answer to God why you refused to live the purpose he had for you.

The last thing you should want is to have any regrets. You don't want to wish you should've done something, but now it's too late. If this is the case, it's time for you to start finding something else you love to do. God gives us many talents and it's up to you to choose which one you want to use.

Jeremiah 29:11 (ESV) - For I know the plans I have for you, declares the LORD, plans for welfare and not for evil, to give you a future and a hope.

If God says he will give you a future and hope, please understand he will do just that. His word does not come back to him void. He is not a God of lies and deceit. However, we are quick to blame God for the things that happen in our lives; when it's actually our own selfishness and foolishness standing in our way.

When we stop standing in our own way, we will be able to re-brand our lives and enjoy our peace.

For so long, I thought I was at peace. Until the day, I opened up my mind and took my blinders off. That's when I realized things weren't all grand. I was a hot mess and ready to change. However, I was looking towards man to find my peace and love. After being constantly disappointed, I had to realize that the only person who could give me the peace and love I was looking for was God. I had to stop putting all my faith in man and start trusting in God to lead the way. I couldn't allow man to continue to steal my peace or joy.

It's easy to give away, but hard to get back. If I knew that a long time ago, I would've never given mine away. I would've protected it a little harder.

When you know better, you do better. I know better now, and refuse to allow anyone else or anything else to come into my life and steal my peace away from me.

It's time to show yourself and God what you're made of. It's time to start living your life for you. You've lived for everyone else. You are a diamond in the rough, and it's time to shine bright like a diamond.

Take the world by the horns and show them who you are. Don't allow the world to take you by the horns and make your life more complicated.

Remember...you are the author of your own story. Can't anyone write it better than you. Now it's time to write the ending of your story. The question is...will it end in peace and love or misery and hate? The choice is yours, but you have to make that decision for you. No one can make that decision but you. Unless, you give them permission; which most people do and don't even realize it.

If you are re-branding yourself to stunt on those who didn't believe in you; you are doing it for the wrong reasons. Although, we want to stunt on those who didn't believe in us; we have changed the way we think, which in turns gives us a different reaction.

Now during this re-branding process, you may lose a lot of friends and family and that's okay. Those are the people who are not suppose to go with you. Everyone in your circle, or still is; isn't supposed to go where God is taking you. Some things are meant just for you.

You have to know what is okay to share with your love ones, and what you need to protect from them. If you give it, they will take it. Be mindful of how much of yourself you give to others. How can you rebrand yourself if there's nothing left to rebrand because, you have given it away to others, who don't have your best interest at heart? It's time to start putting you first, and the only way you can do that is by letting go of your past and focus on your future.

I wish you much success at finding your new peace. Anytime you start to feel like you're getting off track, this is your guide to help you find your way.

No one said life would be easy, and at times we fall off our beaten path. Its okay, you just have to find the will power within yourself and get back on track.

It's time to get out of those dumps and get pumped up. I hope to see you on the other side of your fantastic peaceful life.

About The Author

Tivona Elliott-Clark was born in Wichita, Ks on July 30, 1976. Growing up she loved to write. She found out writing was her get away, from the realities of her life. Becoming desperately ill in 2008, Tivona knew she had to do something to bring in some income, and add some fulfillment to her life.

Still unsure of the path she was supposed to take, God delivered his message telling her to step out on faith. In June 2010, she was diagnosed with Lupus. Finally knowing what was wrong, she refused to allow it to take over her life. In 2010, Tivona started Fast Life Management. Self-publishing her first novel Livin' the Fast Life, Tivona knew she wanted to do more than just write. Not getting the recognition she wanted, she knew she had to learn her craft. Realizing the chaos new author's struggle with in the business, she knew she wanted to make a difference.

In 2013, Tivona republished Livin' the Fast Life and became an author consultant. She now offers services to help authors become self-published. Not only does she offer services for authors, but she also offers services to show you how to get your business on the move. Knowing the importance of business, Tivona wanted to make sure she is able to help others live their dreams. Seeing the reality of her business, she wanted to go a little bit further. In Feb. 2015, she started Fast Life On the Move radio network on Blogtalk Radio. Giving people the opportunity to promote their business, and share their views on topics they can relate to. Not stopping there, in 2016 she partnered with Co-owner Jasmine Night of Bending Reality Magazine, and that partnership became what you now know as Elliott Night Professionals. Doing what they love to do, they found a way to bring the beauty of art to life. Giving artists, musicians, and authors a way of showcasing their work with the world. Although she wears many hats, Tivona never forgets where she comes from. Keeping

God as the head of her life, she continues striving down the path he has before her. No matter what life may throw her way, no weapon formed against her shall prosper. She will continue to empower, enrich, and encourage others to do great things; until God says he's ready for her.

Booking author contact Elliott Night Professionals at

elliottnightprofessional@gmail.com

www.elliottnightprofessionals.com

Other Books available by author

Reflections of Me…Livin' my life through poetry

The Un-Marritable

A Thin Line Between Love & Poetry…Lust & Pain of my Erotic Side

Books Coming Soon

Kenya's Revenge

Livin' the Fast Life Reloaded

The Heart of a Broken Wife

Examples to help get you through

Our Monthly Family Budget

Line Item	Budget	Actual	Difference	Notes:
INCOME				
Earner 1 Income (after tax)			-	
Earner 2 Income (after tax)				
Other Income				
TOTAL INCOME				
EXPENSES				
Vehicles				
Fuel			-	
Household				
Insurance			-	
Dining Out				
Gifts Given				
Clothing				
Child Care			-	
Groceries				
Personal Care				
Medical			-	
Utilities				
Cell Phones				
Mortgage			-	

Be honest with yourself. Treat yourself don't cheat yourself by putting yourself in financial debt.

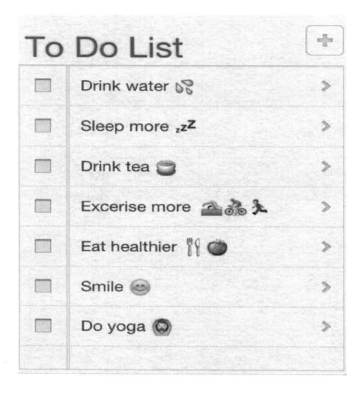

You can do anything you want to do, but here are a few things that may help get you through.

Just for laughs, but this is what living life looks like and you don't have to be ashamed. Live your life abundantly and to the fullest. Laughter is great for the soul.

to do list

1. Make vanilla pudding. Put in mayo jar. Eat in public.
2. Hire two private investigators. Get them to follow each other.
3. Wear shirt that says "Life." Hand out lemons on street corner.
4. Get into a crowded elevator and say "I bet you're all wondering why I gathered you here today."
5. Major in philosophy. Ask people WHY they would like fries with that.
6. Run into a store, ask what year it is. When someone answers, yell "It worked!" and run out cheering.
7. Become a doctor. Change last name to Acula.
8. Change name to Simon. Speak in third person.
9. Buy a parrot. Teach the parrot to say "Help! I've been turned into a parrot."
10. Follow joggers around in your car blasting "Eye of the Tiger" for encouragement.

Questionnaire

What was your best section to this book and why?

How did it help you out?

What goals did you set for yourself?

What did you find out about yourself you didn't know?

What was the most difficult thing you had to face about yourself?

Were you honest with yourself when creating your budget?

Were you able to complete the process successfully?

What was the most challenging process you were faced with during this journey?

Were you able to find your new found peace through this journey?

What questions do you have for the author?

Thank You

I would like to take this time to say thank you to all my readers who believed in me, and have read every book I have published. You guys are awesome, and I'm gratefully thankful for your support.

Thanks to the ENP family for being the best. We will always strive to be the best as a family.

Thanks to Jas and Makala for always having my back and seeing the vision through my craziness. Y'all are the best, and I enjoy working with you both. Let's keep striving for greatness.

To my friends and family, thanks for showing your love and support and always giving me something to write about. Y'all are the best.

Made in the USA
Columbia, SC
16 August 2024

40095257R00046